Ratio Skills Edexcel Maths Higher GCSE 9-1

Revision & Practice

GCSE 9-1

Build confidence with targeted skills practice

First published in the UK by Scholastic, 2017; this edition published 2024

Scholastic Distribution Centre, Bosworth Avenue, Tournament Fields, Warwick CV34 6UQ

Scholastic Ireland, 89E Lagan Road, Dublin Industrial Estate, Glasnevin, Dublin D11 HP5F

www.scholastic.co.uk

A CIP catalogue record for this book is available from the British Library.
ISBN 978-0702-33234-0
Printed by Leo Paper Products, China

Due to the nature of the web, we cannot guarantee the content or links of any site mentioned.

Every effort has been made to trace copyright holders for the works reproduced in this book, and the publishers apologise for any inadvertent omissions.

Author Stephen Doyle
Editorial team Rachel Morgan, Audrey Stokes, Julia Roberts, Haremi Ltd
Series designers emc design ltd
Typesetting York Publishing Solutions Pvt. Ltd. & QBS Learning
Illustrations York Publishing Solutions Pvt. Ltd.
Cover illustration Golden Ratio, david.costa.art/Shutterstock

Notes from the publisher

Please use this product in conjunction with the official specification and sample assessment materials. Ask your teacher if you are unsure where to find them.

The marks and star ratings have been suggested by our subject experts, but they are to be used as a guide only.

Answer space has been provided, but you may need to use additional paper for your workings.

Contents

How to use this book

Inside this book you'll find everything you need to boost your skills in Ratio, Proportion and Rates of change to help you succeed in the GCSE 9–1 Edexcel Higher Mathematics specification. It combines revision and exam practice in one handy solution. Work through the revision material first or dip into the exam practice section as you complete each subtopic. This book will focus on ratio, proportion and rates of change but within your revision you will of course include other topics to ensure overall success. This book gives you the flexibility to revise your way!

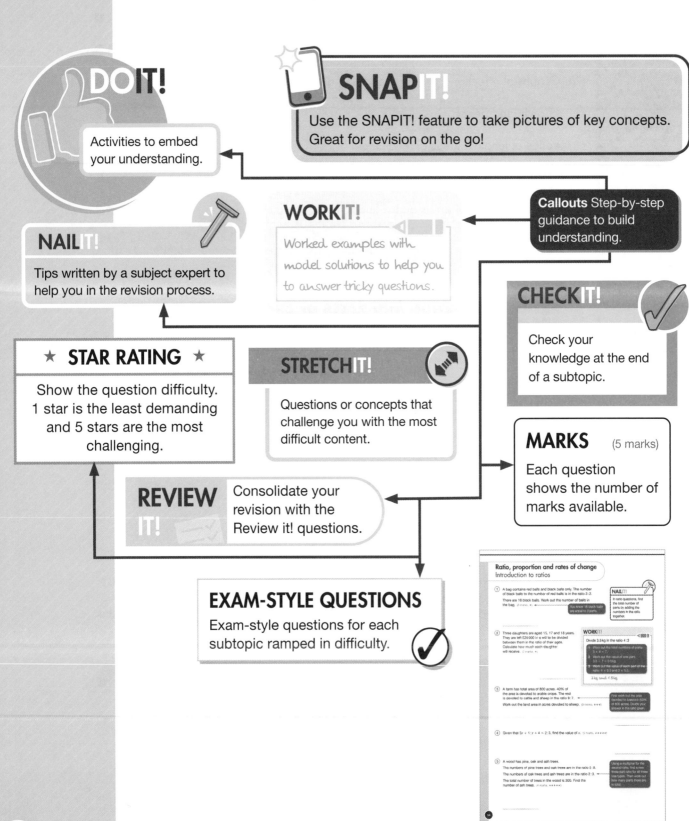

DOIT!
Activities to embed your understanding.

SNAPIT!
Use the SNAPIT! feature to take pictures of key concepts. Great for revision on the go!

Callouts Step-by-step guidance to build understanding.

WORKIT!
Worked examples with model solutions to help you to answer tricky questions.

NAILIT!
Tips written by a subject expert to help you in the revision process.

CHECKIT!
Check your knowledge at the end of a subtopic.

★ STAR RATING ★
Show the question difficulty. 1 star is the least demanding and 5 stars are the most challenging.

STRETCHIT!
Questions or concepts that challenge you with the most difficult content.

MARKS   (5 marks)
Each question shows the number of marks available.

REVIEW IT!
Consolidate your revision with the Review it! questions.

EXAM-STYLE QUESTIONS
Exam-style questions for each subtopic ramped in difficulty.

REVISION

Ratio, proportion and rates of change

Introduction to ratios

Writing ratios

A **ratio** is a comparison between quantities. For example, the ratio of two quantities a and b can be written as $a:b$ or as the fraction $\frac{a}{b}$.

> Ratios are like fractions – cancel them if possible.

Cancel ratios such as $32:48$ by dividing both numbers by the highest number that divides exactly into both. Dividing by 16 simplifies the ratio to $2:3$.

> This is the highest common factor.

The quantities must be in the same units before the ratio is cancelled. If the ratios are in different units (e.g. $1\,kg:200\,g$):

1. Convert both to the smaller unit: $1000\,g:200\,g$.

2. Remove the units: $1000:200$.

3. Cancel the resulting ratio if possible: $5:1$.

WORKIT!

1 On a map a distance of 2 cm represents 5 km. Write the ratio 2 cm : 5 km in the form $1:n$.

> First make the units the same.

$$2\,cm:5\,km = 2:500\,000 = 1:250\,000$$

2 Reduce the ratio $34:6$ to the form $1:n$ where n is a number correct to 2 significant figures.

> To change the 34 into 1, divide it by 34.
> To keep the ratio the same, divide the other side by 34 too.
> Round the value of n to to 2 s.f.

$$34:6 = \frac{34}{34}:\frac{6}{34} = 1:0.1764... = 1:0.18$$

Dividing a quantity into two parts in a certain ratio

SNAP IT! Dividing a quantity in a certain ratio

To divide a quantity in a certain ratio:

1. Add the numbers in the ratio together.

2. Divide this number into the quantity you are dividing up. This gives you what one part represents.

3. Multiply the one part by each number in the ratio in turn.

4. Check that the numbers you get add up to give the original quantity.

NAILIT!

Always check to see if you have to give the value of all the parts or just one of the parts. Always give the answer in the form requested by the question.

WORKIT!

1 £180 is divided in the ratio of 4:5. Find the value of each portion.

Total number of parts = 4 + 5 = 9

1 part = $\frac{£180}{9}$ = £20

So the portions are 4 × 20 = £80 and 5 × 20 = £100 ◄

> Check your answer by adding together the quantities: 80 + 100 = 180.

2 Divide 250 kg in the ratio 0.4:2.8.

0.4 : 2.8 = 4 : 28 = 1 : 7 ◄

> Convert the ratio to whole numbers by multiplying by 10 and then cancelling.

Total number of parts = 1 + 7 = 8

1 part = $\frac{250}{8}$ = 31.25kg

So the portions are 1 × 31.25 = 31.25kg and 7 × 31.25 = 218.75kg

Finding the total being divided in a certain ratio

Sometimes you are given one of the values in the ratio and asked to find the total.

WORKIT!

1 The ratio of the number of boys to girls in a choir is 4:5. There are 16 boys in the choir. How many children are in the choir?

4 parts = 16 children so 1 part = 4 children

Total number of parts 4 + 5 = 9 parts

Total number of children = 9 × 4 = 36

2 A bag contains red and blue balls. The ratio of red balls to blue balls is 2:3. There are ten more blue balls than red balls. Calculate the ◄ total number of balls in the bag.

> You need to use algebra to solve this question, as you do not know how many red or blue balls there are.

Let number of red balls = x, so the number of blue balls = $x + 10$

$\frac{\text{number of red balls}}{\text{number of blue balls}} = \frac{2}{3}$ ◄

> Remember that ratios can also be written as fractions.

$\frac{x}{x + 10} = \frac{2}{3}$

$3x = 2(x + 10)$

$3x = 2x + 20$

$x = 20$

Total number of balls = $x + x + 10 = 50$

3 In a vet's practice, the ratio of the number of dogs seen to the number of cats seen in a week is 5:3.

50% of the dogs are over the age of 5.

60% of the cats are over the age of 5. ◄

> This is a more challenging question. With some questions you have to put in your own numbers.

What percentages of all the dogs and all the cats seen are over the age of 5?

Total number of parts = 5 + 3 = 8

Assume there are 80 dogs and cats in total. ← Pick a number that is divisible by 8, e.g. 80.

Dividing this in the ratio 5 : 3 will give 50 dogs and 30 cats.

Number of dogs over 5 years old = 50% of 50 = 25

Number of cats over 5 years old = 60% of 30 = 18

Number of dogs and cats over 5 years old = 25 + 18 = 43

Percentage of dogs and cats over 5 years old = $\frac{43}{80} \times 100 = 53.75\%$

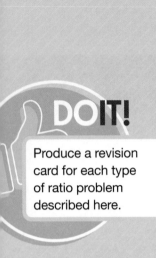

DOIT!

Produce a revision card for each type of ratio problem described here.

✓ CHECKIT!

1 Simplify these ratios.

   a 2:6

   b 25:60

   c 1.6:3.6

2 Express these ratios as simply as possible, without units.

   a 250 g:2 kg

   b 25 m:250 mm

   c 2 cl:1 l

3 Share £400 in the ratio 3.5:2.1.

4 The ratio of the number of girls to the number of boys in a gym is 4:3. There are 180 girls in the gym. Calculate how many children belong to the gym.

5 Three daughters are aged 21, 25 and 29 years. They are left £150 000 in a will to be divided between them in the ratio of their ages.

   Work out how much money the youngest daughter will receive.

6 The number of male and female guests staying at a hotel is in the ratio 5:2.

   40% of the male guests are over the age of 40.

   30% of the female guests are over the age of 40.

   Work out the percentage of all guests under the age of 40.

7 A money box contains 10 p and 20 p coins. The ratio of 10 p coins to 20 p coins is 5:7. There are six more 20 p coins than 10 p coins.

   Calculate the total amount in the money box.

8 In a box of marbles, there are:

   • two times as many blue marbles as red marbles

   • five times as many red marbles as yellow marbles.

   Work out the ratio of blue marbles to red marbles to yellow marbles.

Scale diagrams and maps

On a scale diagram or a map, all the dimensions have been reduced by the same proportion.

For example, a scale drawing of a garden design with a scale of 1 : 50 means that a distance of 1 in any unit on the drawing represents an actual distance 50 times larger. So a pond with a diameter of 5 cm on the drawing would have an actual diameter of 50 × 5 cm = 250 cm (or 2.5 m).

NAILIT!

Always change any measurements into the same units.

WORK**IT!**

A map has a scale of 1 : 50 000. A distance on the map between two villages is 6 cm. What is the actual distance? Give your answer in km.

1 cm on the map is 50 000 cm actual distance.

6 cm on the map is 6 × 50 000 = 300 000 cm actual distance.

$300\,000\,cm = \frac{300\,000}{100}\,m = 3000\,m$ ◄——— Convert 300 000 cm to km.

3000 m = 3 km

Actual distance = 3 km

NAILIT!

Make sure your answer is clearly stated at the end. Sometimes it is best to write a sentence.

WORK**IT!**

An artist is producing a scale drawing of a horse that is 1.75 m tall. The artist has decided to use a scale of 1 : 10. How tall will the horse be on the drawing? Give your answer in centimetres.

1.75 m = 175 cm

Height of horse on drawing = $\frac{1}{10} \times 175 = 17.5\,cm$ ◄——— The scale of 1 : 10 means that the height of the horse needs to be $\frac{1}{10}$ of the horse's actual height.

DOIT!

Work out the actual distance represented by 4 cm on maps at scales 1 : 2500, 1 : 25 000 and 1 : 500 000.

✓ CHECK**IT!**

1 A map has a scale of 1 : 500 000. The actual distance between two cities is 150 km.

   How far apart are the cities on the map? Give your answer in cm.

2 The scale diagram shows an island with a port and two ships A and B out at sea.

a The actual distance between ship A and the port is 10 km. Calculate the scale of the map.

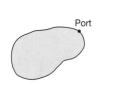

b Work out the actual distance between ships A and B.

Percentage problems

One quantity as a percentage of another

First express the quantities as a ratio in fraction form and then convert this to a percentage by multiplying by 100.

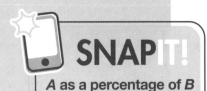

SNAPIT!

A as a percentage of B

Quantity A expressed as a percentage of a quantity B is:

$\frac{A}{B} \times 100\%$

WORKIT!

The theoretical yield of a certain product in a reaction is 0.458 g. The actual yield in an experiment was 0.412 g. Work out the actual yield as a percentage of the theoretical yield. Give your answer to 3 significant figures.

$$\frac{\text{actual yield}}{\text{theoretical yield}} \times 100 = \frac{0.412}{0.458} \times 100$$

$$= 89.9563\%$$

$$= 90.0\% \text{ (to 3 s.f.)}$$

> The actual yield is the numerator and the theoretical yield the denominator. Multiply the fraction by 100 to convert it to a percentage.

Percentage change

Percentage change is worked out in a similar way:

$$\text{Percentage change} = \frac{\text{change}}{\text{original value}} \times 100$$

SNAPIT! Percentage increase/decrease

The change can be an increase or a decrease, so:

$$\text{Percentage increase} = \frac{\text{increase}}{\text{original value}} \times 100$$

$$\text{Percentage decrease} = \frac{\text{decrease}}{\text{original value}} \times 100$$

> Increase = final value − initial value
> Decrease = initial value − final value

WORKIT!

After 1 year a new car originally costing £15 000 is worth £12 000. What is the percentage decrease?

$$\text{Decrease} = \text{initial value} - \text{final value} = 15000 - 12000 = £3000$$

$$\text{Percentage decrease} = \frac{\text{decrease}}{\text{original value}} \times 100 = \frac{3000}{15000} \times 100 = 20\%$$

Adding a percentage onto a quantity

In many situations a certain percentage is added onto a quantity. For example, the price of an article could increase by a certain percentage or you may need to find the price of an article after the VAT has been added on.

> You could work out 20% of 13 500 and then add this on, but there is a quicker way if you can use a calculator.

WORKIT!

1 A car costs £13 500 before VAT. Find the cost of the car after VAT of 20% has been added.

> You are adding 20% to the original amount (i.e. 100%), so you need to find 120% of the original amount, which is the same as multiplying by 1.2.

$$120\% = \frac{120}{100} = 1.2 \quad \leftarrow \text{Work out the multiplier.}$$

> Multiply the original cost by the multiplier.

Price of car including VAT at 20% = 13 500 × 1.2 = £16 200

2 A company's sales in one year were £21 200. The sales the next year increased by 140%. Work out the sales in the second year.

> 100% + 140% = 240%

$$\text{Multiplier} = 240\% = \frac{240}{100} = 2.4$$

Second year's sales = 21 200 × 2.4 = £50 880

Subtracting a percentage from a quantity

Some things go down in price. For example, the value of most cars goes down with age (called depreciation); goods in a sale are often reduced by a certain percentage.

WORKIT!

In a sale, all goods are reduced by 35%. The original price of a pair of shoes was £124. Work out the sale price for the shoes.

$$\frac{35}{100} = 0.35 \quad \text{and} \quad 1 - 0.35 = 0.65 \quad \leftarrow$$

> Work out the multiplier by subtracting the multiplier for 35% from 1.

Sale price = 124 × 0.65 = £80.60

WORKIT!

Jarinda is buying a computer from a shop that offers interest-free credit.

The computer costs £450. She has to pay a deposit of 20% and then a fixed monthly payment over 2 years. Work out how much the fixed monthly payment will be, without using a calculator.

10% of £450 = £45   ←   Divide by 10 to find 10%.

20% of £450 = £90   ←   Double 10% to find 20%.

Deposit = £90

Remainder to be paid over 2 years = 450 − 90 = £360

$$\text{Monthly payment} = \frac{360}{24} = £15$$

NAIL IT!

Use the easiest method that works. Here, you don't need to work out 1%, only 10%, as 20% is a simple multiple of that.

Finding the original value

Sometimes you are given a value after a certain percentage is added and need to find the original value. For example, most shops show a price with the 20% VAT included so you need to calculate the original price before the VAT was added.

> You cannot get the correct answer by finding 20% of £18000 and then subtracting it from £18000. This is because the 20% is of the original price, which is a smaller amount.

> The price before the VAT was 100%, so the price including VAT is 120% of the original price.

> Alternatively, 18000 ÷ 1.2 = 15000.

WORKIT!

1 A car costs £18000 including VAT at 20%. Find the cost of the car before the VAT was added.

120% of original price $= 18000$

10% of original price $= \dfrac{18\,000}{12}$

$= 1500$

100% of original price $=$

$1500 \times 10 = 15000$

Original price $= £15000$

> The price after the discount is $(100 - 15) = 85\%$ of the original price.

2 A tablet computer costs £204 after a discount of 15% in a sale. Calculate the original price of the computer before the discount.

85% of original price $= 204$

5% of original price $= \dfrac{204}{17} = 12$

100% of original price $=$

$12 \times 20 = 240$

Original price $= £240$

> You can spot that $5 \times 17 = 85$.

> When you read the question, decide whether your answer should be larger or smaller than the original value – then check it is when you've finished.

Simple interest

If you put money into a savings account, you will be paid a percentage of the amount in interest. Simple interest means that the amount paid is not added to the original amount and re-invested (for example because it is withdrawn) so the original amount stays the same.

To work out simple interest:

1 Work out the interest that would be paid at the end of one year.

2 Multiply this amount by the number of years the money is invested to give the total interest paid.

WORKIT!

£10000 is invested in an account paying simple interest of 4.5% each year. Find the total amount of interest earned over 5 years.

Amount of interest in one year $= 4.5\%$

of £10000 $= \dfrac{4.5}{100} \times 10000 = £450$

Total interest paid over 5 years $=$

$5 \times £450 = £2250$

DOIT!

> Write down how to find the multiplier for percentage increase and decrease questions.

✓ CHECKIT!

1 In a batch of 300 eggs, 8 eggs were bad. Work out the number of bad eggs as a percentage of the total number of eggs. Give your answer to 2 decimal places.

2 A football manager earns £600000 per year. On the promotion of his team to the Premier League, his earnings increase to £1.1 million per year. Find the percentage increase in his pay. Give your answer to 1 decimal place.

3 Jasmeen earns a salary of £38000 per year in her job as a nurse. She is awarded a pay rise of 3.5%. Find her new salary.

4 In a sale, a mobile phone is reduced by 18%. The sale price is £291.92. Work out the original price.

5 £12000 is invested at an interest rate of 3.5% for 6 years. If simple interest is paid, find the total amount of interest paid over the 6 years.

Direct and inverse proportion

Direct proportion

$y \propto x$ means that y is **directly proportional** to x: as x increases so does y.
For example, doubling x will double y, and halving x will halve y.

The proportional sign can be replaced by an equals sign provided a constant, usually called k is included. k is called the **constant of proportionality** and can be found by substituting known values into the equation for x and y.

For direct proportion, $y = kx$.

If y is directly proportional to x^2 we write $y = kx^2$.

WORKIT!

Write the statement a is directly proportional to the square of b mathematically.

Substitute for a and b to find the value of k.

Substitute k back to find the formula relating a and b.

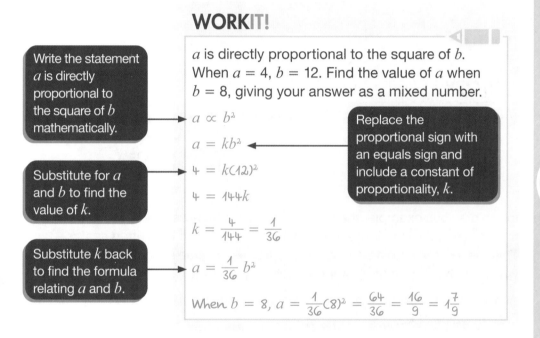

a is directly proportional to the square of b.
When $a = 4$, $b = 12$. Find the value of a when $b = 8$, giving your answer as a mixed number.

$a \propto b^2$

$a = kb^2$

Replace the proportional sign with an equals sign and include a constant of proportionality, k.

$4 = k(12)^2$

$4 = 144k$

$k = \dfrac{4}{144} = \dfrac{1}{36}$

$a = \dfrac{1}{36} b^2$

When $b = 8$, $a = \dfrac{1}{36}(8)^2 = \dfrac{64}{36} = \dfrac{16}{9} = 1\dfrac{7}{9}$

NAILIT!

Always check back to see how the question asks the answer to be given, in this case a mixed number.

Currency problems

Converting between currencies is a particular example of direct proportion. An amount of money in one currency is proportional to the amount in another currency.

WORKIT!

Alegra is on holiday in the USA and sees a watch for $120.

The exchange rate is £1 = $1.45.

a Work out the cost of the watch in pounds.

Cost of watch in pounds $= \dfrac{120}{1.45} = £82.76$

Amount in $ = 1.45 × amount in £.

> Commission is a charge that is a percentage of the value of the amount of money changed.

b When Alegra returns to the UK she has $300 left over which she wants to change back into pounds.

The travel agent offers an exchange rate of £1 = $1.32 without commission. The bank offers an exchange rate of £1 = $1.28 with 3% commission.

Should she use the travel agent or the bank to convert her money back into pounds? Explain your answer.

Travel agent: Amount in pounds $= \frac{300}{1.32} = £227.27$

Bank: Amount in pounds $= \frac{300}{1.28} = £234.38$

> The 3% commission is worked out and then deducted.

Commission $= \frac{3}{100} \times 234.38 = £7.03$

Net amount from bank $= £234.38 - £7.03 = £227.35$

She should use the bank.

Inverse proportion

WORKIT!

It takes 3 men 5 hours to put up a fence. How long would it take 6 men?

> As the number of men doubles, the number of hours halves.

$5 \div 2 = 2.5$ hours

In the previous example, the number of men is **inversely proportional** to the time it takes. If y is **inversely proportional** to x, it can be written as $y \propto \frac{1}{x}$. This means if x doubles, the value of y halves. Inverse proportion can be written with a constant of proportionality, k, as $y = \frac{k}{x}$.

As for direct proportion, if you know a pair of values for x and y, then you can find the value of k.

WORKIT!

Here are some statements. For each statement, write down an equation including a constant.

a a is directly proportional to b. $a = kb$

b R is inversely proportional to I.   Also, $I = \frac{k}{R}$ $R = \frac{k}{I}$

c y is directly proportional to the square of x. $y = kx^2$

d The time of a swing of a pendulum, T, in seconds is directly proportional to the square root of its length, l, in metres. $T = k\sqrt{l}$

e a is inversely proportional to the square root of b. $a = \frac{k}{\sqrt{b}}$

WORKIT!

The pressure, P, of a gas is inversely proportional to its volume, V.
When $V = 12$, $P = 5$.

a Find a formula for P in terms of V.

$P \propto \frac{1}{V}$ so $P = \frac{k}{V}$

$5 = \frac{k}{12}$, giving $k = 60$ ◄———

> Substitute $P = 5$ and $V = 12$ to find the value of k.

$P = \frac{60}{V}$

b Calculate the value of P when $V = 6$.

$P = \frac{60}{V}$

$= \frac{60}{6}$

$= 10$

DOIT!

Design and annotate a revision card for finding the constant of proportionality.

✓ CHECKIT!

1 L is inversely proportional to n.

Carlos says that if you double n, then L will double.

Explain why Carlos is wrong.

2 y is directly proportional to x.

   a Write an equation showing the relationship between x and y.

   b When $y = 8$, $x = 3$. Find the value of y when $x = 4$. Give your answer to 1 d.p.

3 Rosie is on holiday in Greece. She sees a pair of sunglasses costing €120.

She looks on the internet and finds that the cheapest price in the UK is £89.

The exchange rate is £1 = €1.27.

   a In which country are the sunglasses cheaper?

   b Work out the difference in the cost of the sunglasses in the UK and Greece. Give your answer in £.

4 The volume, V cm³, of a sphere is directly proportional to the cube of its radius, r cm.

A sphere with a radius of 2 cm has a volume of 33.5 cm³.

Find the volume of a sphere with a radius of 4 cm.

5 The pressure of a gas, P, is inversely proportional to the volume it occupies, V.

When $V = 1$, $P = 100\,000$. Work out P when $V = 3$. Give your answer to the nearest whole number.

6 $a \propto b^2$ and $a = 96$ when $b = 4$. Find a when $b = 5$.

7 The surface area of a cube, A cm², is directly proportional to the square of the side of the cube, x cm.

   a Write the relationship as an equation and find the value of the constant of proportionality.

   b Hence write down the surface area of a cube with side of length 4 cm.

Graphs of direct and inverse proportion and rates of change

Direct proportion

A graph showing direct proportion is a straight line passing through the origin.

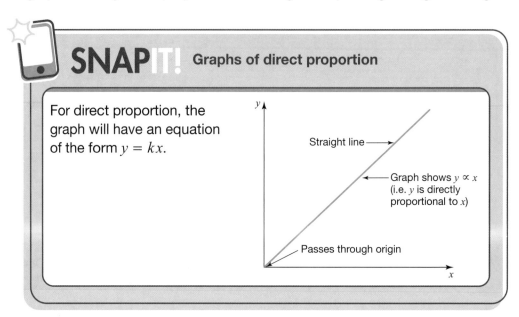

SNAP IT! Graphs of direct proportion

For direct proportion, the graph will have an equation of the form $y = kx$.

Straight line ⟶

Graph shows $y \propto x$ (i.e. y is directly proportional to x)

Passes through origin

This equation is of the form $y = mx + c$, a straight line with gradient m and intercept on the y-axis c. The line passes through the origin, so $c = 0$. So the value of k will be the gradient of the line.

Inverse proportion

The graph showing inverse proportion is a curve of the type shown below.

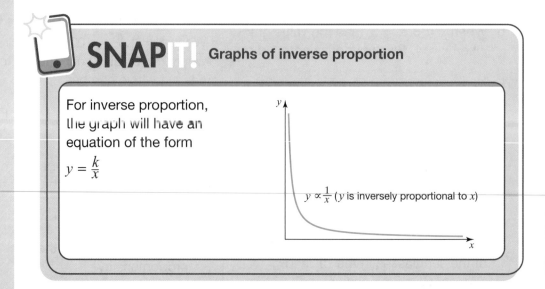

SNAP IT! Graphs of inverse proportion

For inverse proportion, the graph will have an equation of the form

$$y = \frac{k}{x}$$

$y \propto \frac{1}{x}$ (y is inversely proportional to x)

WORKIT!

A graph is drawn of a quantity V against a quantity c.

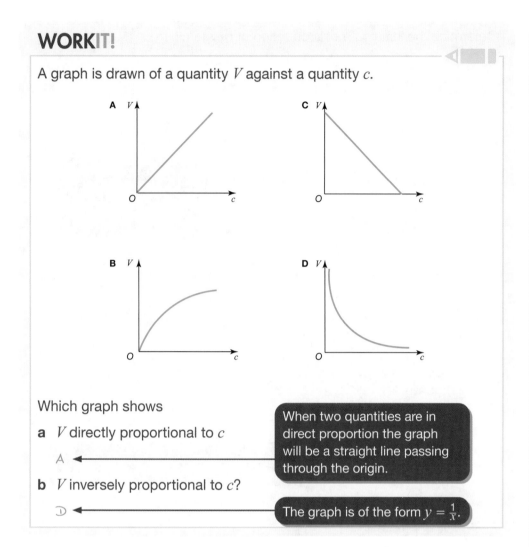

Which graph shows

a V directly proportional to c

A

> When two quantities are in direct proportion the graph will be a straight line passing through the origin.

b V inversely proportional to c?

D

> The graph is of the form $y = \frac{1}{x}$.

Calculating the rate of change from a graph

Graphs used to determine the **rate of change** of a quantity plotted on the y-axis always have **time** along the x-axis.

Suppose an experiment is conducted to investigate the rate of production of oxygen gas during a chemical reaction. The volume of oxygen in m³ is on the y-axis and the time in seconds is on the x-axis. The rate of change of the volume of oxygen is found by measuring the gradient of the graph.

WORKIT!

The volume of oxygen (O_2) produced in a chemical reaction was measured at certain times and gave the following results.

Time (s)	0	50	100	150	200	250	300
Volume O_2 (m³)	0	5.0	10.0	14.8	19.0	22.5	25.0

Plot these results on a graph with volume of oxygen on the y-axis and time on the x-axis.

Determine the initial rate of production of oxygen in m³/s.

Make sure that you label both axes and include the units.

The points are almost in a straight line initially but then they start to bend.

Draw a straight line up to about 200 s and then a smooth curve after that. As the start of the graph is a straight line we can say that the gradient and hence the rate of change of volume of O_2 is constant.

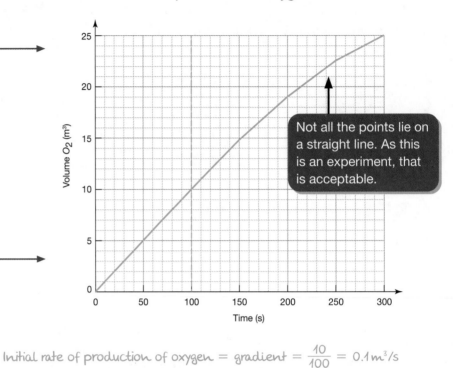

Not all the points lie on a straight line. As this is an experiment, that is acceptable.

Initial rate of production of oxygen = gradient = $\frac{10}{100}$ = 0.1 m³/s

To find the gradient, draw a triangle in the straight section of the graph.

DOIT!

Draw a poster of annotated graphs showing direct and inverse proportion.

CHECKIT!

1 Two quantities, c and V, are in inverse proportion. Which graph shows this?

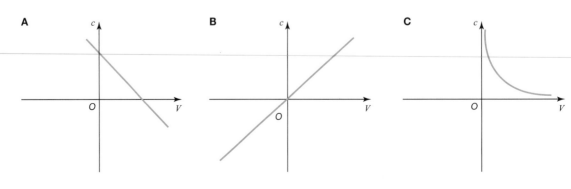

2 Quantity a is directly proportional to quantity b. Which one of the following graphs shows this?

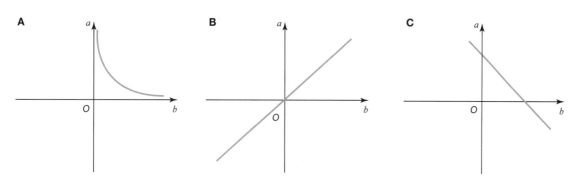

A   B   C

3 The graph shows two quantities, P and V, that are inversely proportional to each other.

The points $A(3, 12)$ and $B(6, a)$ lie on the curve.

Find the value of a.

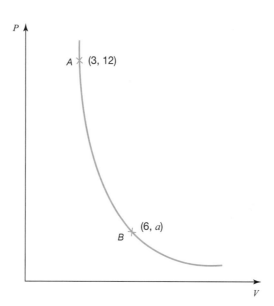

4 The graph shows two quantities x and y which are in inverse proportion to each other.

Find the values of coordinates a and b.

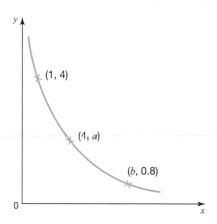

5 For the values below, y is directly proportional to x^2. If a is a positive number, work out the value of a.

x	2	a
y	16	36

Growth and decay

Compound interest

With **compound interest**, the interest is added onto the total amount at the end of each year, which then earns interest too. This means the overall increase is greater each year.

SNAPIT! Compound interest

Amount at the end of n years $= A_0 \times (\text{multiplier})^n$
where n = time period in years, A_0 = original amount of money,
and multiplier $= 1 + \frac{\% \text{ interest rate}}{100}$.

WORKIT!

Jack invests £2000 at 2.75% compound interest. Find the value of the investment at the end of 3 years.

Multiplier $= 1 + \frac{2.75}{100} = 1.0275$ ◄—— Work out the multiplier.

Amount at the end of 3 years $= 2000 \times (1.0275)^3 = £2169.58$

Compound growth

Compound interest is one example of **compound growth**. Other examples can be found in biology. The formula is the same, although the periods of time may be days or hours, not years.

SNAPIT! Compound growth

Amount at the end of n periods of time $= A_0 \times (\text{multiplier})^n$
where n = number of time periods (e.g. years), A_0 = original
amount, and multiplier $= 1 + \frac{\% \text{ rate of growth}}{100}$.

WORKIT!

1 A colony of bacteria increases by 12% each day. There are 4000 bacteria at the start. How many bacteria will there be after 3 days? Give your answer to the nearest whole number.

Multiplier $= 1 + \frac{12}{100} = 1.12$

Amount at the end of 3 days $= 4000 \times 1.12^3 = 5620$ (to 4 s.f.)

2 Algae in a pond grow very quickly in warm weather. The number of algae is 200 000 after 5 days. If the algae grow at a rate of 23% per day, how many algae were there originally?

$\text{Multiplier} = 1 + \frac{23}{100} = 1.23$

$\text{Amount at the end of } n \text{ days} = A_0 \times (\text{multiplier})^n$

$200\,000 = A_0 \times (1.23)^5$

$\frac{200\,000}{(1.23)^5} = A_0$

$A_0 = 71\,040$

Substitute the amount after 5 days and $n = 5$.

SNAP IT!

Compound decay

Amount at the end of n years $= A_0 \times (\text{multiplier})^n$

where n = time period in years, A_0 = original amount and multiplier $= 1 - \frac{\%\ \text{rate of decay}}{100}$.

Compound decay

Compound decay is where a quantity goes down by a certain percentage – like compound growth but in reverse. For example, when you buy a new car it depreciates (i.e. the value goes down with time).

For compound decay, the formula is the same as for compound growth but the multiplier is less than 1.

For decay questions, the multiplier is calculated by **subtracting** the rate from 1.

WORKIT!

Millie buys a new car costing £18 500. The car depreciates at an average rate of 15% per year. Find the value of the car after 4 years, giving your answer to the nearest whole number.

$\text{Multiplier} = 1 - \frac{15}{100} = 0.85$

$\text{Amount at the end of 4 years} = 18\,500 \times (0.85)^4 = 9657.12 = £9657$ (to nearest whole number).

CHECK IT!

1 The equation for compound growth and decay is:

Amount at the end of n units of time $= A_0 \times (\text{multiplier})^n$.

Find the multiplier for each of these situations.

a pond weed in a pond where the growth rate is 5% per week

b bacterial growth where growth rate is 25% per hour

c increase in money if the rate of compound interest is 3.75% per year

d decrease in value if the rate of depreciation is 21%.

2 A motorbike depreciates at a rate of 18% per year. Ben buys a new motorbike costing £9000. How much will his motorbike be worth after 3 years? Give your answer to the nearest whole number.

3 A restaurant chain currently has 4000 restaurants across the UK. It has been expanding by 25% each year. How many restaurants did the company have 3 years ago?

Ratios of lengths, areas and volumes

NAILIT!

If scale factor > 1, the shape will get larger. If scale factor < 1, the shape will get smaller. However, they are both called enlargements!

Scale factors

When two shapes are **similar**, they are identical in shape but not in size. One shape is simply an **enlargement** of the other. A missing length on one of the shapes can be found by considering the scale factor:

Scale factor for enlargement $= \frac{\text{big}}{\text{small}}$

Scale factor for reduction $= \frac{\text{small}}{\text{big}}$

WORKIT!

P and Q are similar triangles. Find the length of the side marked x on triangle Q.

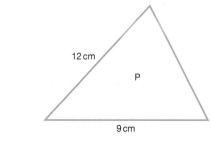

You are finding the smaller length, so find the scale factor for the reduction.

Multiply the side on P corresponding to x by the scale factor.

$\text{Scale factor} = \frac{\text{corresponding side of Q}}{\text{corresponding side of P}} = \frac{8}{12} = \frac{2}{3}$

$x = \frac{2}{3} \times 9 = 6\,cm$

You can prove two triangles are similar by comparing the ratios of corresponding sides.

NAILIT!

You need to compare **all** the pairs of corresponding sides to prove triangles are similar. You can also prove similarity by showing that all the angles are the same.

WORKIT!

Identify whether these triangles are similar.

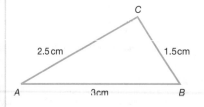
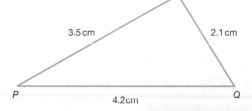

Work out the ratio for each corresponding pair of sides.

$\frac{PQ}{AB} = \frac{4.2}{3} = 1.4$ $\frac{QR}{BC} = \frac{2.1}{1.5} = 1.4$ $\frac{PR}{AC} = \frac{3.5}{2.5} = 1.4$

The ratio is the same, so the triangles are similar.

Scale factors for area and volume

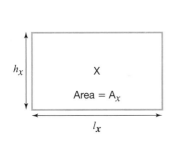

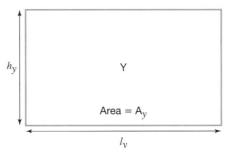

For rectangles X and Y, scale factor for length, $k = \dfrac{h_y}{h_x} = \dfrac{l_y}{l_x}$

Scale factor for area $= \dfrac{h_y \times l_y}{h_x \times l_x}$

$= \dfrac{h_y}{h_x} \times \dfrac{l_y}{l_x} = k^2$ or the square of the scale factor for length.

Similarly, the scale factor for volume is equal to the cube of the scale factor for length.

SNAPIT!

2D and 3D scale factors

For two similar shapes or solids with a scale factor k:

- scale factor for area $= k^2$

- scale factor for volume $= k^3$

NAILIT!

You must always check that you are told, or can prove, that two shapes or solids are similar before using scale factors.

WORKIT!

Prove that triangle *ABC* is mathematically similar to triangle *DBE*.

$AD = 3\,cm$, $DB = 6\,cm$ and $AC = 8\,cm$.

Work out the area of triangle *DBE*.

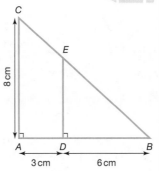

Angle CAB = angle EDB = 90°

Angle ABC = angle DBE (same angle)

Angle ACB = 180° − angle CAB − angle ABC

(angle sum in a triangle)

Angle DEB = 180° − angle EDB − angle DBE (angle sum in a triangle)

So angle ACB = angle DEB

All the angles are the same, so triangles ABC and DBE are similar. ◄—— First prove that the triangles are similar.

Area of triangle $ABC = \dfrac{1}{2} \times b \times h = \dfrac{1}{2} \times 9 \times 8 = 36\,cm^2$

Scale factor $= \dfrac{DB}{AB} = \dfrac{6}{9} = \dfrac{2}{3}$ ◄—— Work out the scale factor from the ratio of corresponding sides.

$\dfrac{\text{Area } DBE}{\text{Area } ABC} = (\text{scale factor})^2 = \left(\dfrac{2}{3}\right)^2 = \dfrac{4}{9}$

Area $DBE = \dfrac{4}{9} \times$ Area $ABC = \dfrac{4}{9} \times \dfrac{1}{2} \times 9 \times 8 = 16\,cm^2$ ◄—— Use the fact that the triangles are similar to write the ratio of the areas.

NAILIT!

If you are not told two triangles are similar, you must first prove that they are similar.

WORKIT!

Two solid spheres, P and Q, are mathematically similar.
The ratio of the volume of P to the volume of Q is 8:125.

a Find the ratio of the radius of sphere P to the radius of sphere Q.

$$\frac{V_P}{V_Q} = \left(\frac{r_P}{r_Q}\right)^3$$

> Scale factor for volume = (scale factor for length)^3.

$$\frac{8}{125} = \left(\frac{r_P}{r_Q}\right)^3$$

$$\frac{r_P}{r_Q} = \sqrt[3]{\frac{8}{125}} = \frac{2}{5}$$

b The surface area of sphere Q is 37.5 cm². Show that the surface area of sphere P is 6 cm².

> Scale factor for area = (scale factor for length)^2.

$$\frac{A_P}{A_Q} = \left(\frac{r_P}{r_Q}\right)^2 = \left(\frac{2}{5}\right)^2 = \frac{4}{25}$$

$$A_P = \frac{4}{25} \times A_Q = \frac{4}{25} \times 37.5 = \frac{150}{25} = 6$$

Surface area of sphere P is 6 cm².

DOIT!

Make up some scale factor questions then come back to them tomorrow.

✓ CHECKIT!

1 Triangles A and B are similar. Find the length of the side marked x on triangle A. Give your answer as a mixed number.

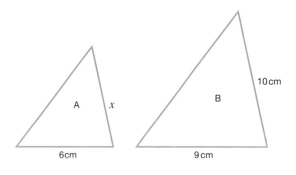

6 cm   9 cm   10 cm

2 Two cylinders are mathematically similar. Cylinder A has a volume of 27 cm³ and cylinder B has a volume of 64 cm³.

The surface area of cylinder B is 96 cm².

Show that the surface area of cylinder A is 54 cm².

3

5 cm   5 cm
A   B   C
8 cm
E
D

ABC and AED are straight lines. Lines BE and CD are parallel. Angle ACD = 90°.

CD = 8 cm, BC = 5 cm and AB = 5 cm.

a Work out the length of side BE.

b Work out the area of triangle ABE.

Gradient of a curve and rate of change

The gradient of a curve changes with position so you need to know where the gradient is to be measured. Usually the x coordinate is given, which determines where on the curve to find the gradient.

With rate of change graphs, time is always plotted on the x-axis.

The instantaneous rate of change

The **instantaneous rate of change** is the gradient of the tangent drawn at that point.

For example, this graph shows how the velocity of an object changes with time.

The gradient of a velocity–time graph gives the acceleration. To find the acceleration at time $t = 10\,\text{s}$, work out the gradient of the tangent:

Acceleration at $10\,\text{s}$ = gradient
$= \dfrac{12 - 4}{16 - 6} = \dfrac{8}{10} = 0.8\,\text{m/s}^2$

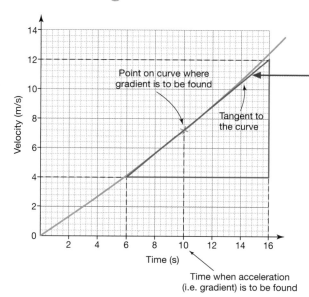

Point on curve where gradient is to be found

Tangent to the curve

Time when acceleration (i.e. gradient) is to be found

The tangent is the straight line that just touches the curve.

STRETCH IT!

Use the same method to find the gradient of a curve from a graph by drawing in a tangent.

The average rate of change

The **average rate of change** is the gradient of the line drawn between two points on the curve. Each point corresponds to a certain time.

Average acceleration between $6\,\text{s}$ and $16\,\text{s}$ = gradient = $\dfrac{8}{10}$
$= 0.8\,\text{m/s}^2$

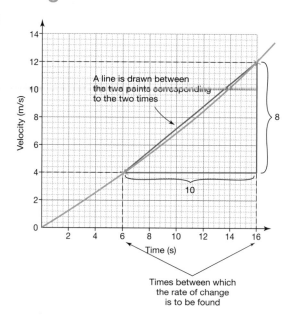

A line is drawn between the two points corresponding to the two times

Times between which the rate of change is to be found

WORKIT!

The graph shows how the height of grain in a large hopper changes with time, t, when it is being filled with grain.

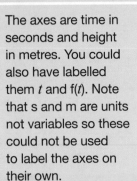
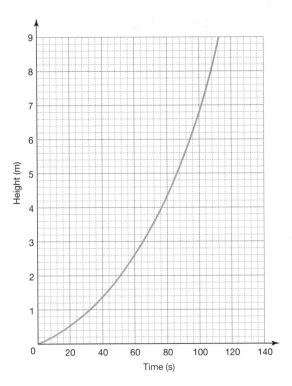

a Find the instantaneous rate of change of height when $t = 80$ s.

Draw a tangent to the curve at $t = 80$ s and find its gradient.

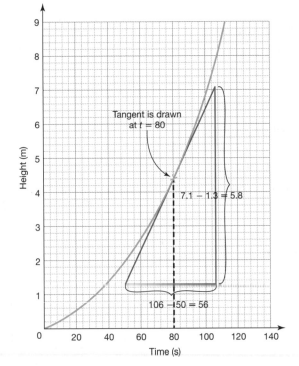

Tangent is drawn at $t = 80$

$7.1 - 1.3 = 5.8$

$106 - 50 = 56$

Instantaneous rate of change of height = gradient = $\dfrac{5.8}{56}$

= 0.1 m/s (to 1 s.f.)

b Find the average rate of change of height between $t = 40\,s$ and $t = 80\,s$.

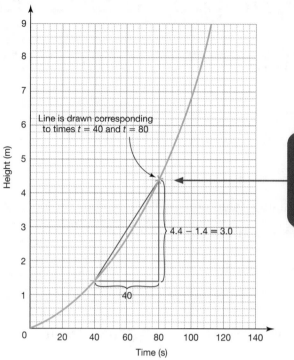

Line is drawn corresponding to times $t = 40$ and $t = 80$

$4.4 - 1.4 = 3.0$

40

Join the points on the curve at $t = 40\,s$ and $t = 80\,s$ with a straight line and find its gradient.

Average rate of change of height between $t = 40s$ and $t = 80s$
$$= gradient = \frac{3}{40} = 0.08\,m/s \text{ (to 1 s.f.)}$$

DOIT!

Draw and annotate distance–time and velocity–time graphs to show instantaneous and average gradients and what they represent.

✓ CHECKIT!

1 An accelerating particle has the velocity–time graph shown on the right.

a State what the gradient of the curve represents.

b Find the average acceleration of the particle between 2 s and 6 s.

c Find the time when the instantaneous acceleration is the same as the average acceleration calculated in part b.

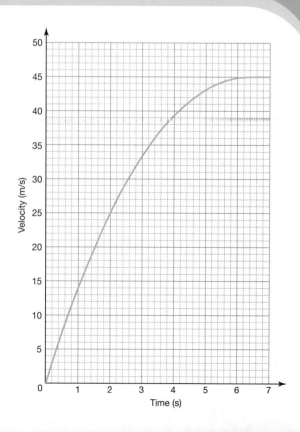

Converting units of areas and volumes, and compound units

Converting areas and volumes

Converting between m² and cm²

A 1 m by 1 m square has an area of 1 m².

This is the same as a 100 cm by 100 cm square, which has an area of 100 × 100 = 10 000 cm².

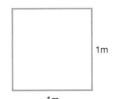 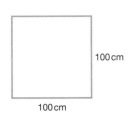

> Note that 1 m² does not equal 100 cm².

> We've given one answer in standard form and one as a decimal. Both are acceptable.

So 1 m² = 10 000 cm² and 1 cm² = $\frac{1}{10\,000}$ m² = 1×10^{-4} m².

Similarly, 1 cm² = 100 mm² and 1 mm² = $\frac{1}{100}$ cm² = 0.01 cm².

Converting between m³ and cm³

Similarly, a cube of side 1 m has a volume of 1 m³, and a cube of side 100 cm has a volume of 100 × 100 × 100 = 1 000 000 cm³.

So 1 m³ = 1 000 000 cm³ and 1 cm³ = $\frac{1}{1\,000\,000}$ m³ = 1×10^{-6} m³.

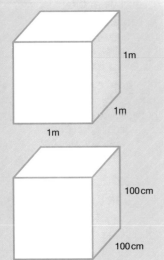

Similarly, 1 cm³ = 1000 mm³ and 1 mm³ = $\frac{1}{1000}$ cm³ = 0.001 cm³.

WORKIT!

1 Convert:

  a 250 cm³ to m³

    $250\,cm^3 = 250 \times 10^{-6}\,m^3 = 2.5 \times 10^{-4}\,m^3$

  b 1.500 m² to cm²

    $1.5\,m^2 = 1.5 \times 10\,000\,cm^2 = 1.5 \times 10^4\,cm^2$

Compound units

> The per symbol (i.e. /) acts like a divide sign, and can tell you information about the formula. For example, one unit of speed is km/h, which tells you a distance in km is divided by a time in h.

Compound units are made up of two units (for example m/s, km/h, g/cm³). Quantities such as speed, density, pressure, rate of pay and price per unit have compound units. These are all worked out by dividing one quantity with one unit by a different quantity with a different unit.

SNAP IT! Compound units

Compound units include:

$$\text{speed} = \frac{\text{distance}}{\text{time}} \qquad \text{unit m/s or km/h}$$

$$\text{density} = \frac{\text{mass}}{\text{volume}} \qquad \text{unit g/cm}^3 \text{ or kg/m}^3$$

$$\text{pressure} = \frac{\text{force}}{\text{area}} \qquad \text{unit N/m}^2 \text{ or Pa } (= \text{N/m}^2)$$

$$\text{rate of pay} = \frac{\text{pay}}{\text{time}} \qquad \text{unit £/h, £/month, £/year}$$

$$\text{price per unit} = \frac{\text{price}}{\text{number of units}}$$
unit for price on the top could be pence or pounds
unit on the bottom could be g, kg, ml, tonne, etc.
compound unit p/g, £/kg, etc.

Speed is worked out using the formula $\qquad \text{speed} = \frac{\text{distance}}{\text{time}}$

You need to be able to rearrange this

formula to get: distance = speed × time $\qquad \text{time} = \frac{\text{distance}}{\text{speed}}$

STRETCH IT!

When speed is in a particular direction, it is called **velocity**. For more on this see pages 25–7.

NAIL IT!

You need to learn this formula as it will not be given. To remember the formula for speed, think of the units for speed, which are m/s or km/h: distance divided by time.

WORK IT!

1 Dhaya is driving her car at an average speed of 80 km/h.

a Work out her speed in metres per second, correct to the nearest whole number.

$80 \text{ km/h} = 80 \times 1000 \text{ m/h}$

$\qquad = \dfrac{80 \times 1000}{60 \times 60} \text{ m/s}$

$\qquad = 22.22 \text{ m/s}$

$\qquad = 22 \text{ m/s (to nearest whole number)}$

NAIL IT!

Always look back at the question to check how accurate the answer needs to be.

b Calculate the time in minutes it would take her to drive a distance of 30 km at this average speed.

> Rearrange speed = $\frac{\text{distance}}{\text{time}}$ to give time = $\frac{\text{distance}}{\text{speed}}$

$\text{time} = \dfrac{\text{distance}}{\text{speed}} = \dfrac{30}{80} = 0.375 \text{ h}$

$0.375 \text{ h} = 0.375 \times 60 \text{ minutes} = 22.5 \text{ minutes}$

NAIL IT!

Always look at the units required for the answer. This tells you whether you need to change any of the units for the values in the calculation.

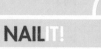

The answer needs to be in N/m², so convert the area from cm² to m².

NAIL IT!

Remember that time is not metric.

2 Using the formula pressure = $\frac{\text{force}}{\text{area}}$ work out the pressure in N/m² when a force of 500 N acts on an area of 20 cm².

$$20\,cm^2 = 20 \times 10^{-4}\,m^2 = 2 \times 10^{-3}\,m^2$$

$$pressure = \frac{force}{area} = \frac{500}{2 \times 10^{-3}} = 250\,000\,N/m^2$$

3 A train covers a distance of 29 km in 45 minutes. Calculate its average speed in km/h. Give your answer to the nearest whole number.

$$45\,mins = \frac{45}{60}\,h = 0.75h$$

$$speed = \frac{distance}{time} = \frac{29}{0.75} = 38.67\,km/h = 39\,km/h \text{ (to nearest hour)}$$

DO IT!

Look up the 'speed formula triangle' on the internet. Produce similar triangles for density and pressure.

CHECK IT!

1 The diagram shows a solid block of wood.

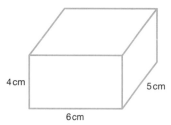

4 cm

5 cm

6 cm

a Find the total surface area of the block in:

i mm²   ii m².

b Find the volume of the block in m³.

2 A bar of gold has a volume of 600 cm³ and a mass of 1.159 kg. Work out the density of gold in g/cm³ giving your answer correct to 3 decimal places.

3 A block of steel with a volume of 1 m³ is melted and used to create lots of ball bearings. The volume of each ball bearing is 0.5 cm³. How many ball bearings could be made?

4 A car is travelling with an average speed of 50 km/h. Find this speed in m/s. Give your answer correct to 2 decimal places.

5 Kieran drove from Manchester to Bristol. It took him 4 hours at an average speed of 70 km/h.

Mary drove by the same route and took 5 hours.

a What was Mary's average speed for her journey?

b If Mary took a different route, how might this affect your answer to part a?

1 In a sale the price of a dress was reduced by 20% to £76.80. What was the original price of the dress?

2 The area of floating pond weed that grows on the surface of a pond in t days is $A\,m^2$, where

$A_0 = 5$

$A_{t+1} = 1.02A_t$

Work out the area covered by the pond plants in

a 1 day   b 3 days.

Give your answers to 2 decimal places.

3 y is inversely proportional to x.

When $x = 2.5$, $y = 4$.

Find the value of y when $x = 5$.

4 The ratio of the number of students studying history in Year 11 to those not studying history is $2:7$. There are 54 students studying history. How many students are there in Year 11?

5 The price of a house in a certain town has increased by 120% over the last 10 years.

The original price of the house was £220 000. How much is the house worth now? Give your answer to the nearest £5000.

6 £2000 is invested at an interest rate of 2.5% for 5 years. Work out how much money is in the account after 5 years if the interest paid is

a simple interest

b compound interest (to the nearest penny).

7 Tom goes on holiday to China. The exchange rate is £1 = 8.55 yuan.

He changes £400 into yuan.

a Work out how many yuan he should get.

After his holiday, Tom has 800 yuan left over which he wants to change back into pounds.

The travel agent offers an exchange rate of £1 = 8.6 yuan with 2.5% commission.

The post office offers an exchange rate of £1 = 8.9 yuan with no commission.

b Should Tom change his money at the travel agent or the post office? Explain your answer.

8 A company is owned by Joshua, Amy and Luke, in the ratio of $3:5:7$.

Any profits are shared in this ratio.

When the profits for a certain year were shared, Luke received £4000 more than Amy.

Work out the total profit for the year.

9 Two solids are mathematically similar. Solid A has a surface area of $25\,cm^2$ and solid B has a surface area of $4\,cm^2$.

The volume of solid A is $10\,cm^3$.

Find the volume of solid B.

10 The number of male and female members of a swimming club is in the ratio $7:4$.

25% of the male members are junior members.

10% of the female members are junior members.

Work out the percentage of junior members in the club, giving your answer to the nearest integer.

11 A bronze alloy is made by mixing copper and tin. The masses of the copper and tin are in the ratio $9:1$.

The density of copper is $8.9\,g/cm^3$.

The density of tin is $7.3\,g/cm^3$.

Work out the density of the bronze alloy. Give your answer to 1 decimal place.

EXAM PRACTICE

Ratio, proportion and rates of change
Introduction to ratios

(1) A bag contains red balls and black balls only. The number of black balls to the number of red balls is in the ratio 3:2.

There are 18 black balls. Work out the number of balls in the bag. (3 marks, ★) ◄

> You know 18 black balls are equal to 3 parts.

....

(2) Three daughters are aged 15, 17 and 18 years. They are left £25 000 in a will to be divided between them in the ratio of their ages. Calculate how much each daughter will receive. (3 marks, ★)

WORKIT!

Divide 3.5 kg in the ratio 4:3

1. Work out the total numbers of parts: 3 + 4 = 7.
2. Work out the value of one part: 3.5 ÷ 7 = 0.5 kg.
3. Work out the value of each part of the ratio: 4 × 0.5 and 3 × 0.5.

2 kg and 1.5 kg

....

(3) A farm has total area of 800 acres. 40% of the area is devoted to arable crops. The rest is devoted to cattle and sheep in the ratio 9:7. ◄

Work out the land area in acres devoted to sheep. (3 marks, ★★★)

> First work out the area devoted to livestock (60% of 800 acres). Divide your answer in the ratio given.

....

(4) Given that $3x + 1:x + 4 = 2:3$, find the value of x. (3 marks, ★★★★★)

....

(5) A wood has pine, oak and ash trees.

The numbers of pine trees and oak trees are in the ratio 5:8.

The numbers of oak trees and ash trees are in the ratio 2:3. ◄

The total number of trees in the wood is 300. Find the number of ash trees. (4 marks, ★★★★★)

> Using a multiplier for the second ratio, find a new three-part ratio for all three tree types. Then work out how many parts there are in total.

....

Scale diagrams and maps

(1) The scale on a map is 1 : 50 000.

Two towns are 10 cm apart on the map.

What is their actual distance apart?
Give your answer in km. (2 marks, ★)

....

NAILIT!

When changing a map scale to a ratio, make sure that the two quantities in the ratio are changed into the same units. For example,
1 cm : 500 m = 1 cm : 50 000 cm
= 1 : 50 000.

(2) A map is drawn to a scale of 1 : 40 000. Find the actual length, in km, of a straight road of length (★)

a 2.3 cm (1 mark)   **b** 3 mm (1 mark) ◄───

Multiply each of these lengths by 40 000 and then change the units.

....

[Total: 2 marks]

(3) On a scale drawing of a garden, the length of a path whose actual distance is 40 m is 5 cm. Find the scale of the drawing in the form 1 : n where n is an integer. (3 marks, ★★)

....

STRETCHIT!

If you photocopied this page at A3 scale, the enlargement could be expressed by the ratio 1 : $\sqrt{2}$.

How would this affect the answer you get in Question 4?

(4) The map shows a port and a gas rig.

The actual distance from the port to the gas rig is 12 km.

By taking a measurement from the map, work out the scale of the map.

Give your answer in the form 1 : n where n is an integer. (3 marks, ★★)

....

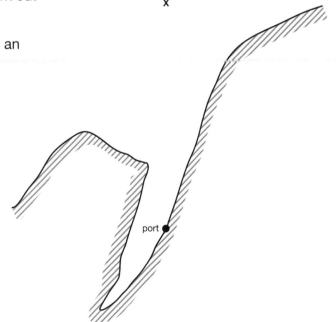

Percentage problems

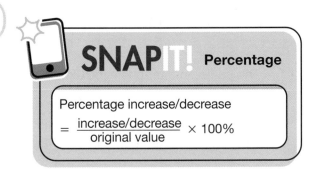
(1) A store selling bikes increases the price of a bike from £350 to £385. Find the percentage increase. (2 marks, ★★)

....

(2) A football manager initially earns £600 000 per year. On the promotion of his team to the Premier League his earnings increase to £1.1 million per year. Find the percentage increase in his pay to 1 decimal place. (2 marks, ★★)

....

STRETCHIT!

The Whizzie skateboard has been reduced by 20%, from £22 to £17.60. Karl bought his Zoomtown board somewhere else, also for £17.60. He tells Katie, 'At full price, Whizzie skateboards are 20% more expensive than Zoomtown ones'. Is he right?

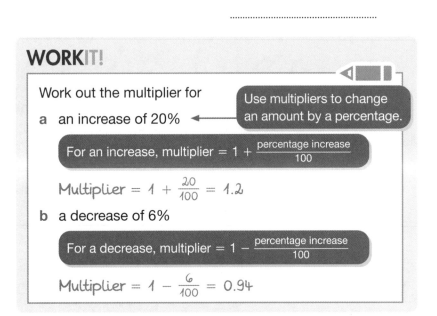

WORKIT!

Work out the multiplier for

> Use multipliers to change an amount by a percentage.

a an increase of 20%

> For an increase, multiplier = $1 + \dfrac{\text{percentage increase}}{100}$

Multiplier $= 1 + \dfrac{20}{100} = 1.2$

b a decrease of 6%

> For a decrease, multiplier = $1 - \dfrac{\text{percentage increase}}{100}$

Multiplier $= 1 - \dfrac{6}{100} = 0.94$

(3) After 3 years a caravan originally costing £25 000 has decreased in value by 28%. What is its new value? (2 marks, ★★)

....

(4) The price of a motorbike after a reduction of 12% is £14 300. Find the original price of the motorbike. (3 marks, ★★★)

> Start by saying that 88% of the original price is £14 300.

....

(5) Fran invests £8000 at an interest rate of 2.8% for 4 years. If simple interest is paid, find the total amount of interest paid over the 4 years. (2 marks, ★★★)

....

Direct and inverse proportion

1 The pressure of a gas, P, is directly proportional to its temperature, T. (★★★)

   a Write the above statement as an equation. (1 mark)

> **NAILIT!**
>
> When y is directly proportional to x you can write $y = kx$.
>
> When y is inversely proportional to x you can write $y = \frac{k}{x}$

....

   b The pressure is 200 000 Pascals when the temperature is 540 Kelvin.

     Find the value of pressure when the temperature is 200 Kelvin. Give your answer to the nearest whole number. (3 marks)

> Use the pair of values to find the value of the constant.

....
                         [Total: 4 marks]

2 The cost of building a circular garden pond is directly proportional to the square of the radius of the pond. The cost when the radius is 3 m works out at £480.

Find the cost of building a circular pond with a radius of 4 m. Give your answer to the nearest whole number. (4 marks, ★★★★)

....

3 A quantity c is inversely proportional to another quantity h.

When $c = 3$, $h = 12$ (★★★)

   a write a formula for c in terms of h.

     (1 mark)

             b calculate the value of c when $h = 15$.

             (2 marks)

....

                         [Total: 3 marks]

(4) Emma goes to France on holiday. (★★★)

a She changes £350 into euros at an exchange rate of £1 = €1.15

Work out how many euros she gets. (1 mark)

....

b When she returns she still has €80.

She changes this back to pounds at an exchange rate of £1 = €1.11.

How many pounds does she get? Give your answer to the nearest penny. (2 marks)

....

c How much would she have saved if she had only changed the money that she needed for the holiday? (3 marks)

....

[Total: 6 marks]

Graphs of direct and inverse proportion and rates of change

① Which one of these graphs shows that y is directly proportional to x? (1 mark, ★★★)

A 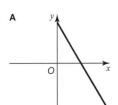 B 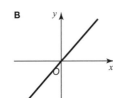 C 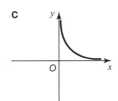 D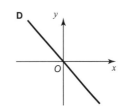

....

② The pressure, P, of a gas is inversely proportional to the volume, V. Which graph correctly shows this statement? (1 mark, ★★★)

A 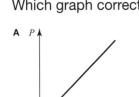 C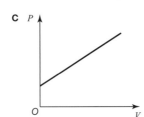

B 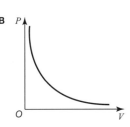 D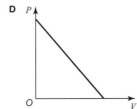

....

③ In a chemical experiment, the mass of contents in a flask was measured every minute and the loss in mass calculated. The results are shown in the table. (★★★★)

Time (minutes)	0	1	2	3	4	5	6	7
Loss in mass (g)	0	9.8	19.6	24.5	26.6	27.7	28	28

a Plot the results on the grid. (2 marks)

b Work out the initial rate of loss of mass in

   i g/minute (2 marks)

   .... g/minute

   ii g/second. (1 mark)

   .... g/second

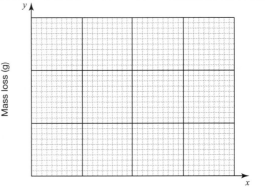

Mass loss (g)

Time (minutes)

[Total: 5 marks]

Growth and decay

(1) The population of a town is 150 000. Each year the population increases by 6%. (★★★★)

> As the population is increasing, the multiplier will be greater than 1.

    a What will the population be 3 years from now? (2 marks)

    ....

    b After how many years will the population have risen to over 200 000? Give your answer to the nearest year. (2 marks)

    ....

[Total: 4 marks]

(2) Jenny buys an electric car. The car costs £21 000 and it depreciates at a rate of 12% each year. What will be the car's value after 4 years? Give your answer to the nearest whole number. (3 marks, ★★★★)

> Depreciation means that the multiplier will be less than 1.

....

(3) A radioactive isotope halves its activity every 12 seconds.

The initial activity of a sample of the isotope was 100 units.

Find the activity after 2 minutes. Give your answer to 1 significant figure. (4 marks, ★★★★★)

....

Ratios of lengths, areas and volumes

1 These two triangular prisms are mathematically similar. (★★★★)

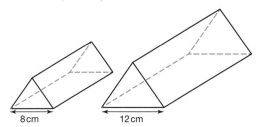

8 cm   12 cm

a Find the scale factor for the volume of the larger prism in relation to the smaller one. (2 marks)

Work out the scale factor for the lengths first, then use this to find the scale factor for volume.

....

b The area of the triangular cross-section of the small prism is 10 cm². Find the area of cross-section of the large prism. (2 marks)

.... cm²

c The volume of the large prism is 450 cm³. Find the volume of the small prism. Give your answer to the nearest whole number. (2 marks)

.... cm³

[Total: 6 marks]

(2) These two solid cuboids are mathematically similar.

The volume of the larger cuboid is 195.3% of the volume of the smaller cuboid.

Calculate the height, h, of the larger cuboid.
Give your answer to the nearest cm. (4 marks, ★★★★★)

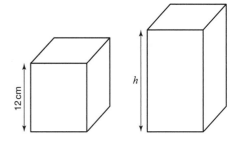

12 cm

h

....

(3) *XY*, *TU* and *WZ* are parallel lines. *YZ*, *YW* and *XZ* are straight lines.

$YU = 10\,\text{cm}$, $UZ = 5\,\text{cm}$ and $UT = 3\,\text{cm}$. (★★★★★)

a Calculate the length of

    i *XY* (1 mark)   ii *WZ* (1 mark)

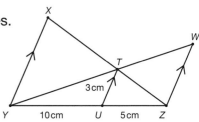

X

W

T

3 cm

Y   10 cm   U   5 cm   Z

.... cm   .... cm

b Find the ratio of the areas of triangles *TYX* and *TWZ*.
Give your answer in the form $n:1$ (2 marks) ◄————

If the area of triangle *TWZ* is 1 unit, n represents the comparable area of *TYX*.

....

[Total: 4 marks]

Gradient of a curve and rate of change

(1) The velocity–time graph shows a car's motion for 90 seconds. (★★★★★)

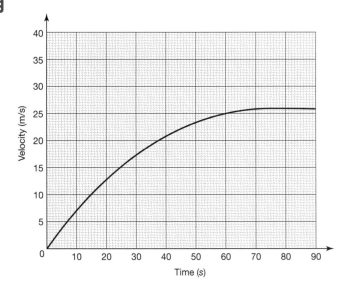

a Find the acceleration during the first 15 seconds. (2 marks) ◄—— Draw a triangle to find the gradient over 0–15 seconds (velocity in relation to time).

....

b Work out the instantaneous acceleration at 45 seconds. (2 marks)

....

c Work out the average acceleration over the first 70 seconds. (2 marks)

....

d At a certain time the instantaneous acceleration is equal to the average acceleration over the first 70 seconds. (2 marks)

Find the time in seconds when this happens.

....

[Total: 8 marks]

Converting units of areas and volumes, and compound units

① The formula to work out pressure is pressure $= \dfrac{\text{force}}{\text{area}}$.

Calculate the pressure produced by a force of 200 N acting on an area of 0.4 m². Give your answer in N/m². (1 mark, ★★)

> The answer requires the force to be in Newtons and the area in m² so no conversions are needed.

....

② Calculate the pressure in Newton/m² if a force of 500 Newtons acts on an area of 200 cm². (2 marks, ★★★)

....

③ The formula for density is density $= \dfrac{\text{mass}}{\text{volume}}$.

Copper has a density of 8.92 g/cm³.

Find the mass in grams of a length of copper wire with a volume of 12 cm³. Give your answer to the nearest gram. (2 marks, ★★★)

....

NAILIT!

Compound units are made up of two units: for example m/s for speed, km/h for speed, g/cm³ for density. When entering units into a formula, check whether the values are in the units needed for the final answer. If not, you will need to convert your answer to the correct units.

④ A picture has a length of 167 cm and a width of 54 cm.

Joshua wants to work out the area of the picture in m² correct to 2 decimal places.

Here is his working.

Area = length × width = 167 × 54 = 9018 cm²

Area in m² $= \dfrac{9018}{100} = 90.18$ m²

Joshua's answer is wrong.

Explain what he has done wrong and work out the correct area in m². (2 marks, ★★★)

....

⑤ Umar drove for 2 hours at 60 km/h. He then drove for 3 hours at 80 km/h.

Work out his average speed for the journey. (3 marks, ★★★★)

....

ANSWERS

Answers

For full worked solutions, visit:
www.scholastic.co.uk/gcse

Revision answers

Introduction to ratios p.8

1 **a** 1:3   **b** 5:12   **c** 4:9
2 **a** 1:8   **b** 100:1   **c** 1:50
3 £250, £150
4 315 members
5 £42 000
6 62.9%
7 £5.70
8 10:5:1

Scale diagrams and maps p.9

1 30 cm
2 **a** 1:500 000 **b** 6 km

Percentage problems p.12

1 2.67%   3 £39 330   5 £2520
2 83.3%   4 £356

Direct and inverse proportion p.15

1 Inverse proportion means that if one quantity doubles the other quantity halves.
2 **a** $y = kx$ **b** 10.7
3 **a** cheaper in the UK
   b £5.49 cheaper in the UK
4 268 cm³
5 33 333 (to nearest whole number)
6 150
7 **a** $A = 6x^2$, $k = 6$ **b** 96 cm²

Graphs of direct and inverse proportion and rates of change p.18

1 Graph C
2 Graph B
3 $a = 6$
4 Equation connecting x and y is $y = \frac{k}{x}$
   When $x = 1$, $y = 4$ so $4 = \frac{k}{1}$ so $k = 4$
   The equation of the curve is now $y = \frac{4}{x}$
   When $x = 4$, $y = \frac{4}{4} = 1$ so $a = 1$
   When $y = 0.8$, $0.8 = \frac{4}{x}$ giving $x = 5$ so $b = 5$.
   Hence $a = 1$ and $b = 5$.
5 $y = kx^2$
   When $x = 2$, $y = 16$ so $16 = k \times 2^2$ giving $k = 4$.
   $y = 4x^2$
   Hence $36 = 4x^2$ so $x = 3$
   $a = 3$

Growth and decay p.21

1 **a** 1.05   **c** 1.0375
   b 1.25   **d** 0.79
2 £4962 (to nearest whole number)
3 2048

Ratios of lengths, areas and volumes p.24

1 $6\frac{2}{3}$ cm
2 $\frac{V_A}{V_B} = \frac{27}{64} =$ (scale factor)³, so scale factor $= \frac{3}{4}$
   $\frac{A_A}{A_B} =$ (scale factor)² $= \frac{9}{16}$
   So $A_A = \frac{9}{16} \times 96 = 54$ cm²
3 **a** Triangles *ABE* and *ACD* must be proved similar:
       BE parallel to *CD*, all the corresponding angles in both triangles are the same.
       BE = 4 cm
   b 10 cm²

Gradient of a curve and rate of change p.27

1 **a** The gradient represents the acceleration.
   b 5 m/s²
   c 3.9 s

Converting units of areas and volumes, and compound units p.30

1 **a** **i** 14 800 mm²
          ii 0.0148 m²
   b 0.000 12 m³
2 1.932 g/cm³ (to 3 d.p.)
3 2 000 000
4 13.89 m/s (to 2 d.p.)
5 **a** 56 km/h
   b The distance will not be the same, so the average speed will be different.

Review it! p.31

1 £96
2 **a** 5.10 m²
   b 5.31 m²
3 $y = 2$
4 243 students
5 £485 000
6 **a** £2250
   b £2262.82
7 **a** 3420 yuan
   b travel agent (travel agent £90.69; post office £89.89)
8 £30 000
9 0.64 cm³
10 20%
11 8.7 g/cm³

Exam practice answers

Introduction to ratios p.34

1   30
2   £7500, £8500, £9000
3   210 acres
4   $x = \frac{5}{7}$
5   144

Scale diagrams and maps p.35

1   5 km
2   **a** 0.92 km   **b** 0.12 km
3   1 : 800
4   1 : 200000

Percentage problems p.36

1   10%
2   83.3%
3   £18000
4   £16250
5   £896

Direct and inverse proportion p.37

1   **a** $P = kT$ **b** 74074 Pascals (to nearest whole number)
2   £853 (to nearest whole number)
3   **a** $c = \frac{36}{h}$ **b** 2.4
4   **a** €402.50   **b** £72.07 (to nearest penny)   **c** £2.50

Graphs of direct and inverse proportion and rates of change p.39

1   B
2   B
3   **a**

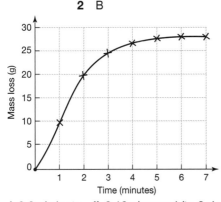

b   **i** 9.8 g/minute   **ii** 0.16 g/second (to 2 d.p.)

Growth and decay p.40

1   **a** 178652   **b** 5 years
2   £12594
3   0.1 (to 1 s.f.)

Ratios of lengths, areas and volumes p.41

1   **a** 3.375 or $\frac{27}{8}$
    b 22.5 cm²
    c 133 cm³ (to nearest whole number)
2   $h = 15$ cm (to nearest cm)
3   **a** **i** 9 cm **ii** 4.5 cm   **b** 4 : 1

Gradient of a curve and rate of change p.43

1   **a** $\frac{2}{3}$ m/s²
    b 0.26 m/s²
    c 0.37 m/s²
    d 34 s

Converting units of areas and volumes, and compound units p.44

1   500 N/m²
2   25000 N/m²
3   107 g (to nearest g)
4   He has worked out the area in m² by dividing the area in cm² by 100, which is incorrect.
    There are 100 × 100 = 10000 cm² in 1 m², so the area should have been divided by 10000.
    Correct answer:
    area in m² = $\frac{9018}{10000}$
    = 0.9018
    = 0.90 m² (to 2 d.p.)
5   72 km/h

SCHOLASTIC

GCSE Skills

Build confidence with targeted skills practice

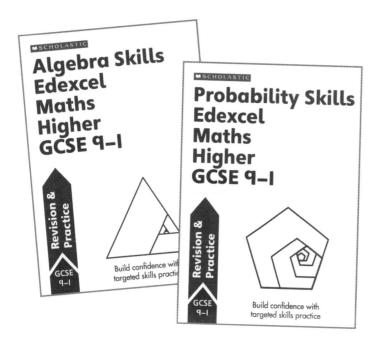

Revise GCSE Maths topics in greater depth

- Clear and focused explanations of tricky topics

- Questions that offer additional challenge

- Deepen understanding and apply knowledge

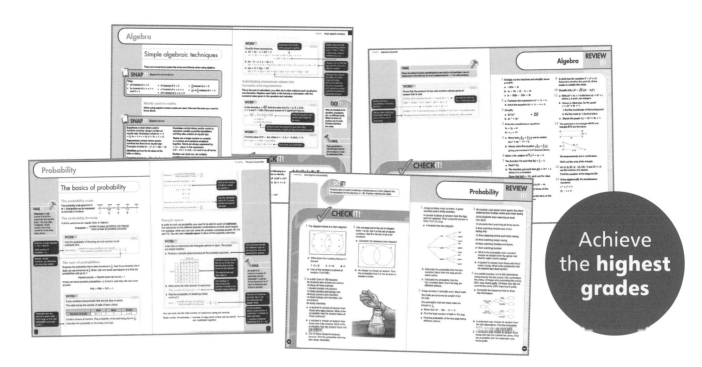

Achieve the **highest grades**

Revision & Practice › **10-Minute Tests** › **National Tests** › **Catch-up & Challenge**

Find out more at **www.scholastic.co.uk/learn-at-home**